A gift from Evelyn Brookins,
Publisher
For more information about this book
please visit
www.lullabyforachild.com
or call: 949-916-5086

Lullaby for a Child

a poem by Doris Peel

Lullaby for a Child speaks and sings of God's ever-present loving care for everyone and everything. Its comforting message brings healing, protection and peace to all God's kids – young and old.

With much gratitude to Quintan Craig, Orange County Song and Dance Company, to Erik Przytulski, Veronica Eckstein, Jerry Adamowicz, James Staunton and Nektarios Tradas for their stellar professional contributions.

Dedicated to Jack Brooklyn Mickelthwate, who inspired and motivated us.

Evelyn Brookins
Carl Symons
August 2005
Laguna Hills, California

www.lullabyforachild.com

All the little birds have gone
in their nests to sleep

And out in folds I cannot see

sleep the woolly sheep

All the flowers that grow by day

pink and blue and white

Are just as safe in darkest dark

For lamb and bird
and smallest flower
white or pink or blue

Are held all round by God

"I am loving while you sleep in bed or nest or fold"

"All My darlings every one

in My arms I hold"

"I am loving while you sleep

"Every flower and bird and lamb

and you My child as well"

"O every child of Mine I keep close to Me each hour"

"So bide you quietly through the night

like bird and lamb and flower"

All the little birds have gone
in their nests to sleep,
and out in folds I cannot see
sleep the woolly sheep.

All the flowers that grow by day
pink and blue and white
are just as safe in darkest dark
as in the brightest light.

For lamb and bird and smallest flower,
white or pink or blue,
are held all round by God who says
"I am loving you!"

"I am loving while you sleep
in bed or nest or fold,
all My darlings, every one
in My arms I hold."

"I am loving while you sleep
softly now and still,
every flower and bird and lamb
and you, My child, as well."

"O every child of Mine I keep
close to Me each hour,
so bide you quietly through the night
like bird and lamb and flower."

Lullaby for a Child a poem by Doris Peel

Arranged for piano or guitar

Book Acknowledgments:

Lullaby for a Child by Doris Peel used by permission from The Christian Science Publishing Society

Music used by permission from The Christian Science Board of Directors

Illustrated by James Staunton, San Diego, California

Book and CD designed by Nektarios Tradas, ARTWORX, San Diego, California

---

CD Acknowledgments:

Poem read by Evelyn Brookins

Father and son dialogue by Carl Symons and Quintan Craig

Music used by permission from The Christian Science Board of Directors

Lullaby for a Child by Doris Peel used by permission from The Christian Science Publishing Society

Music arranged and performed by Erik Przytulski and sung by Veronica Eckstein and Erik Przytulski

Musical interlude composed and performed by Jerry Adamowicz

Children's Chorus, Orange County Song and Dance Company, Westminster, California:

Alex Bachman	Mollie Rae Craig
Jakie Batinga	Quintan Craig
Kelela Rose Batinga	Lauren Delaney
Jenae Burrows	Marissa Holliday

Directed by Linda Hoppus, Cherie Batinga and Sandy Hines

Recorded at Adamo's Recording Studio, Westminster, California, May 2005
Recording Engineer: Jerry Adamowicz

Copyright and Publishing info:

Published by *Jessica Driver's* Reading Aloud Institute™
23871 Willows Drive, Suite 162, Laguna Hills, California 92653
877.587.5579
www.readingaloudinstitute.com

ISBN: 0-9771355-0-0

©2005 by *Jessica Driver's* Reading Aloud Institute™

First edition August 2005
Printed in the United States of America

HLSITTaCUbDRRBENZ
tSSSSSZZ.
MWIHOPmV
ILonpscm